WEST KENT COLLEGE

Your Questions
Answered

ALCOHOLISM:

Yours Questions Answered

LIZ HODGKINSON

WARD LOCK

A WARD LOCK BOOK

First published in the UK 1995
by Ward Lock
Wellington House
125 Strand
LONDON
WC2R OBB

A Cassell Imprint

Distributed in the United States
by Sterling Publishing Co., Inc.
387 Park Avenue South, New York, NY 10016-8810

Distributed in Australia
by Capricorn Link (Australia) Pty Ltd
2/13 Carrington Road, Castle Hill NSW 2154

A British Library Cataloguing in Publication Data block for this book
may be obtained from the British Library

ISBN 0 7063 7402 9
Design and computer make-up by Tony & Penny Mills
Printed and bound in Great Britain by Biddles

Liz Hodgkinson is a journalist and author who has contributed to most leading
publications in the UK, including The Times, Guardian, Independent, Daily Mail, Cosmopolitan, and
Woman's Own. She broadcasts extensively on radio and television, has presented 'Woman's
Hour' and edits the magazine Top Woman. She is the author of more than 25 books on a
variety of subjects.

Contents

Introduction

There is no doubt that, nowadays, more alcoholic beverages than ever before are being consumed, and by a much wider cross-section of people. In the UK and the USA, until the 1950s, few people, apart from the wealthier classes, ever drank wine. Now every corner shop, every supermarket, is groaning with wine from all over the world and it is an unusual social occasion at which alcoholic drinks are not offered. Indeed, so rare has a non-alcoholic occasion become that, if wine is not on offer, one feels that something is missing.

Children and teenagers regularly drink wine at their parent's and friends' houses and many sixth-form schools and colleges now have their own bars. In addition, in the many television series depicting the lives of ordinary working people, the characters are frequently shown drinking wine at home.

This would not have happened a few decades ago, when it was not considered 'respectable' to drink at home and all regular drinking had to take place outside the house. My grandmother, for example, never entered a drinking establishment in her entire life and partook of just one small sherry and a glass of port at Christmas, neither of which she appeared to enjoy. For the rest of the year, the port and sherry bottles sat untouched in the cupboard and my grandfather, who did drink, had to resort to the local pub for his quaffing, as did most working men in those days.

How have these changes in drinking habits affected the incidence of alcoholism, or problem-drinking as it is now more usually referred to in the UK? Has the easy availability of alcoholic drinks and the increasingly liberal drinking laws encouraged more people to succumb to temptation and drink more than is good for them?

Drunken hooligans, so-called 'lager-louts', are frequently featured in the press and on television, but is this merely media hype or a genuine problem? And how many of these people go on to become addicted drinkers or to have problems with alcohol?

These are all questions that this book sets out to answer. Alcoholism is an emotive, a pejorative, word, and the disorder is surrounded by many myths. The popular impression of an alcoholic is of someone who is dead drunk all the time, always unsteady on their feet, and who desperately reaches for a drink first thing in the morning. But what is the truth about alcoholism –

and why do some people drink more than is good for them? Why do some people quite literally drink themselves to death?

It is common knowledge that alcohol is intoxicating and can be addictive, yet many people perhaps most, can drink sociably without addiction ever setting in or drinking becoming a problem. Most people enjoy the occasional alcoholic drink, but can take it or leave it, and do not panic unduly if one is not available.

For some people, however, alcohol consumption becomes a serious matter. They literally seem unable to live without it. It has been estimated by those working in alcoholism and addiction services, that between 1 and 2 million people in the UK and 25–30 million in the USA may be alcoholics.

Drinking to excess is a serious problem, not only because it impairs physical health, but also because it affects behaviour, perception and judgement. It increases the likelihood of road accidents, violence, child abuse and marital difficulties, and is frequently implicated in crime.

In fact, it is estimated by the UK Government agency, Alcohol Concern, that 50 per cent of the people currently languishing in prison are there because of offences related to alcohol.

What makes the issue even more difficult is the almost raffish glamour which surrounds alcohol abuse, and the sophisticated culture which has evolved around vintage wines, single malt whiskies and fine brandies. Wine experts are lauded as celebrities, their books sell in millions, and the owners of vineyards and breweries are often part of the aristocracy.

In some ways, alcohol is considered one of the adornments, one of the finer things, of life. A good wine graces a dinner party; vintage champagne makes people more convivial on social occasions. What is the connection between the confident sophistication of a wine expert, elegantly sipping a rare vintage, and the vagrant who buys strong cider and drinks in the streets?

When it comes to alcoholism, the differences may be more of degree than kind. Everyone would like to be able to drink in moderation, to enjoy alcohol as one of the good things of life, and yet, for reasons we shall be examining in this book, some seem unable to control their intake. These people come from all parts of the social spectrum. Indeed, alcoholism may eventually turn many previously respectable people into down-and-outs.

Alcohol is not, at least in Western societies, an illicit drug, although, for some people, it can become like such a drug. Where is the dividing line between the enjoyment of intoxicating beverages and uncontrolled addiction to them?

Until recently, most of the images surrounding alcohol abuse have been entirely negative: Hogarth's *Gin Lane*, with its degraded people getting high on cheap alcohol, the down-and-outs of Skid Row, unsavoury-looking vagrants drinking meths or pure alcohol. Such people have always been depicted as weak, shiftless and irresponsible.

In the USA and the UK and other countries connected with British imperialism, there has certainly always been a somewhat puritanical attitude towards drinking. In the nineteenth and early twentieth centuries in the UK there were even temperance establishments that sold beer-like concoctions containing no alcohol, and children were encouraged to sign the pledge and join the Band of Hope, vowing that they would never, ever touch the demon drink.

In the USA, in the 1920s, there was Prohibition, whereby in certain states at least, the manufacture and sale of alcohol was banned altogether, much as some other drugs are today.

Of course, neither the Band of Hope nor Prohibition succeeded in wiping out alcohol use.

Americans became very adept at illegally distilling 'bootleg' liquor and it was during this time that cocktails were invented, to make inferior alcohol drinkable, or to disguise the alcohol content. Also during this time there was a rise in patent medicines with a high alcohol content.

In the UK, people continued to drink, but quite often more or less secretly, which is why so many men in the past resorted to the public house to drown their sorrows.

In many northern European countries, such as Norway, Denmark and Sweden, the attitude was the same. Drink was evil, a demon – and decent people did not partake of it. (In Mediterranean countries, however, wine has always been part of the culture and it is a rare occasion when it is not consumed).

This Calvinistic idea that alcoholic beverages were not respectable, not for the God-fearing, has had a profound effect on alcoholism recognition and treatment. Until very recently, to be an alcoholic, to be unable to control one's drinking, was considered too shameful to be admitted. Alcoholics themselves denied their problem, as did those around them.

If there was such a terrible thing as a drinker in the family, this was kept a closely guarded secret from outsiders. The alcoholic would deny the problem as strongly as the immediate family. Doctors were, until recently, extremely reluctant to recognize, diagnose, or treat drink-related problems. One of the reasons for this, it has been suggested, is that many doctors were themselves alcoholics but didn't want anyone to know.

It would be reassuring to say that this attitude has now completely disappeared, that the moral strictures surrounding alcohol abuse have vanished forever. Unfortunately, this is not the case. There remains more than a vestige of the notion that someone who drinks to excess is somehow a moral reprobate, a kind of criminal.

This lingering attitude is at last beginning to disappear, thanks partly to the willingness of many celebrities to admit to an alcohol problem, and to the availability of books about the subject. Also, treatment of alcohol-related problems is improving all the time.

As a result of these changing attitudes, the subject is increasingly coming into the open and the problem is being faced fairly and squarely. Humane treatment centres and programmes are being established and, at last, serious research is being carried out into alcohol use and abuse.

There is still much controversy surrounding the whole subject of alcohol addiction, and much discussion about whether alcoholics can ever become controlled drinkers or must abstain for life. There is also a great deal of argument about the causes of alcoholism: whether it is genetic, the result of social factors, or related to a particular alcoholic, or addictive, personality.

During the course of this Question and Answer book, all aspects of alcohol-related problems will be examined and explanations given about how they can most successfully be recognized and treated. Along the way, I hope that it will be possible to replace many of the myths and misunderstandings still surrounding alcohol, with knowledge and understanding about a serious problem which can have far-reaching effects, not only for those affected by problem drinking, but for all who come into contact or live with them.

Questions
and
Answers

1 About Alcohol

Q Is alcohol a stimulant or a depressant?

Although alcohol is known to make people merry and more outgoing, it is actually a depressant of the central nervous system. It is an anaesthetic drug which has the ability to damp down all body systems, including the brain. The 'merriness' which comes from drinking a few glasses of wine or beer is due to the removal of inhibitions. Alcohol puts a block on the inhibitory centres of the brain, which allows more outgoing behaviour than normal. However, although alcohol appears to have a stimulating effect initially, depression often sets in when the drinker sobers up.

Q What is the 'active ingredient' of an alcoholic drink?

This ingredient is the same, whether we are talking about cider, beer, spirits, rare vintage wines or cheap lager. Ethyl alcohol, which is created during the fermentation of sugars by yeast, is the substance responsible for the intoxicating effect.

Q How do we measure the strength of an alcoholic drink?

Since 1980, in the European Community (EC), the alcohol content of drinks has been measured as percentage Alcohol by Volume (ABV). As a result of a European directive which came into force in 1989, ABVs must be displayed on the labels of all cans and bottles, and on the price lists in public houses, restaurants and wine bars.

Low-alcohol beers have an ABV of 1·2 per cent or less while alcohol-free beers are below 0·5 per cent. Average beer strength is about 3·5 per cent, although super-strength lagers can go up to 9·5 per cent. Cider averages about 4·2 per cent, table wine 11–13 per cent, sparkling wine 12 per cent, sherry and port 17–18 per cent and whisky 40 per cent.

Q What is a unit of alcohol?

A unit of alcohol is 8–10 ml (0·28–0·35 oz) of absolute alcohol. This is the amount contained in 284 ml (½ UK pt) of ordinary beer, a small glass (142 ml/¼ UK pt) of table wine or a single measure (25 ml/approx. ⅙ UK gill) of spirits.

Q Why does alcohol have more effect on an empty stomach?

There is a simple reason. Alcohol enters the blood-stream through the walls of the stomach, and it can do this more quickly when the stomach is empty. The presence of food in the stomach slows down the absorption of alcohol and delays its effects.

Q Which are the most alcoholic beverages?

Spirits have the highest alcohol content, although, because of the high carbon content, sparkling wines enter the bloodstream far more quickly than still wines. Spirits mixed with carbonated drinks, such as colas, are also quickly absorbed.

Q How is alcohol detoxified in the body?

The main detoxifying organ is the liver, which generally copes very well. Human beings are unique in having a specific enzyme – alcoholase – in the body which neutralizes and deals with alcohol. A by-product of this is the formation of acetaldehyde.

A small proportion of any alcohol ingested is eliminated from the body via the urine, breath and perspiration; the remainder is oxidized, i.e. it combines with oxygen in the blood to release heat and energy (calories). Unlike food, however, it is burnt up almost exclusively in the liver, which is why the liver is one of the first organs to suffer from the effects of prolonged heavy drinking.

As a general rule, it takes the liver 1 hour to detoxify 1 unit of alcohol. The more slowly you drink, the more effectively the liver can deal with the alcohol.

Q Is it true that women cannot take as much alcohol as men?

This depends on what you mean by 'take'. Women tend to get drunk far more quickly than men, and their systems become saturated with alcohol more easily than those of men, for three reasons:

1. Women usually weigh less than men and, as a result, the alcohol in their bodies becomes more concentrated;

2. Women have more body fat, which is impenetrable to alcohol, and less body fluid to dilute the alcohol;

3. Alcohol seems to be metabolized differently at different stages of the menstrual cycle, although no one is yet completely sure of the mechanism behind of this.

Some women, however, can drink just as much as men, and the latest Danish research by the Institute of Preventative Medicine, Copenhagen in 1994, which gave 40 units a week as a safe limit, did not differentiate between men and women. It seems that, generally, women in the UK drink less than men: an average of 5·4 units a week, compared with about 16 for men (The Brewers' Society, 1994). Figures for the USA are very similar.

The point is that there are great variations in the amounts individuals can drink without being ill, having a hangover or suffering from long-term side-effects.

Q Is it true that alcohol makes women sexier?

The famous rhyme by Ogden Nash goes: 'Candy is dandy, but liquor is quicker'. Scientific research has now added credence to the old belief that, if you want to seduce a woman, first get her drunk. Recent studies by the Biomedical Research Centre in Helsinki have discovered that alcohol produces small but significant increases in testosterone (the hormone responsible for the sex drive in both men and women). However, it only seems to have this effect in women, for reasons not yet understood.

By decreasing inhibitions, alcohol may lead to overtly sexier behaviour, and thus make some women appear more sexually assertive. This effect, however, is lost when the alcohol evaporates from the system and women may then regret the sexy behaviour which they displayed while under its influence.

Q **It is said that 21 units for a man and 14 units a week for a woman are a safe amount. Is this true, and how were these figures calculated?**

In 1979, when the idea of 'units' was first mooted, it was said that 56 units a week was about right. This figure came down and down until the figures of 14 for women and 21 for men were adopted as a 'safe' level. Some Danish research suggests that 40 units a week is unlikely to harm the body of a reasonably healthy man or woman but other research suggests that harmful effects are directly related to the amount of alcohol consumed.

In the early 1990s, these units were seriously questioned and, now, the idea of what constitutes 'moderate' drinking is once again under review.

In France, the idea of 21 units for men and 14 for women a week would be ludicrous – many

French men drink at least a bottle of wine a day. Nevertheless, most people working in the field of alcoholism are agreed that the so-called 'sensible drinking guidelines' can do no harm, to perception, health or behaviour.

These guidelines, of course, apply only to regular drinking. You may well suffer harmful effects if you drink 14 or 21 units in one sitting!

Drinkers are also recommended to have at least two alcohol-free days a week, so that alcohol consumption does not creep up to the level where you cannot go even a day without it.

2 Alcohol and Health

Q What happens when alcohol enters the body?

Alcohol is a drug which depresses the central nervous system, damping down all body systems. This is why it can numb both mental and physical pain. When it is swallowed it travels to the stomach and small intestine, where it is absorbed into the bloodstream through the gut walls.

The amount of alcohol passing into the blood, and the rate of its absorption, depends on the quantity and nature of the beverages ingested and the amount of food in the stomach. Fizzy alcoholic drinks, e.g. champagne, enter the bloodstream extremely quickly, causing an uplifting effect with almost the first sip.

For women, the effects of alcohol can also relate to the menstrual cycle: alcohol is absorbed more rapidly just before menstruation and during ovulation. Women who take the contraceptive pill may find that alcohol is absorbed and metabolized more slowly, and therefore stays in the system for longer.

Once in the blood, alcohol travels to all areas of

the body, including the brain, within minutes. The depressant effect of alcohol on the central nervous system means that 'messages' take longer to travel to and from the brain along the nerves. The result of this is a dulling and slowing of the brain's responses and reaction times, and thoughts and co-ordination suffer. As more alcohol is consumed, it thus becomes increasingly difficult to carry out complex mental and physical tasks, and the functioning of all body systems becomes impaired.

Q Are there any other factors determining the effect of alcohol?

The immediate effects depend on the level of alcohol in the bloodstream at any one time. This is known as the blood alcohol concentration (or BAC). The BAC varies according to sex, weight, body composition and speed of drinking. On average, the liver can metabolize and detoxify 1 unit of alcohol per hour.

The following shows how alcoholic beverages, if drunk in quick succession can affect adult behaviour:

1.   568 ml (1 UK pt) of beer or its equivalent (a double whisky, two glasses of wine) can result in general unsteadiness and certainly increases the likelihood of an accident.

2. 852 ml (1½ UK pt) of beer, three whiskies
    or three glasses of wine usually increases
    cheerfulness, by damping down the inhibi-
    tory centres of the brain, and increases the
    impairment of perception and judgement.

3. 2·84 l (5 UK pt) of beer, ten whiskies or 1l
    (1¾ UK pt) of wine results in loss of self-
    control, slurred speech and often quarrelsome
    behaviour.

4. 525 ml (¾ bottle) of spirits can cause obliv-
    ion, sleepiness and coma, and, drunk straight
    down, may even cause death. The effect on
    people who have drunk large amounts over a
    long period of time is lessened as tolerance to
    the drug increases, although some chronic
    drinkers often find that their tolerance
    decreases again because their livers can no
    longer process the alcohol.

Q What causes hangovers?

These are caused partly by a kind of poisoning
and partly by the dehydration and fall in blood
sugar levels which alcohol consumption causes.

The main causes of the poisoning are substances
known as 'congeners' – impurities which are
present in all alcoholic drinks, but particularly in

darker-coloured drinks, such as brandy and red wine. Dehydration occurs because alcohol is a diuretic, i.e. it stimulates the production of urine. Alcohol also stimulates the production of insulin, and this is responsible for the reduction in blood sugar levels. These low levels are the cause of drowsiness, weakness, trembling, faintness and hunger. In addition, the acid in the drinks can cause stomach upsets.

There is no real cure for a hangover, although some people swear by evening primrose oil. Drinking large amounts of water and orange juice helps, although time is the only real solution. The 'hair of the dog' is especially dangerous because, in addition to keeping BAC levels raised, it can lead to dependence on alcohol.

Q How does alcohol affect health?

All mind-altering chemicals have both a physical and a mental effect. The most drastic, such as alcohol, and heroin or cocaine, have what the American medical profession term a 'quick ageing effect' (according to Dr Joseph Cruse in *Painful Affairs*). This is thought to be due to the speeding up of the process by which the body deals with alcohol, along with other processes, including degeneration. It is a feature of alcoholics that they all look much older than they are, as well as having a variety of physical diseases which eventually become irreversible. Faces, hands and bodies also age markedly when where is alcohol abuse on a chronic scale.

A question was once posed in a newspaper as to why one never saw a bald vagrant. An expert in alcohol-related problems replied that, although vagrants look old, many of them are actually still quite young and this is why they often have masses of hair. In fact, many homeless people are chronic alcohol abusers and it is often their dependence on alcohol, rather than anything else, which has brought them to their sorry state. Conversely, many people who find themselves on the streets turn to alcohol for some relief.

Alcoholics and problem drinkers tend to look much older than they really are. Alcohol is the opposite of an elixir of youth – especially as problem drinkers also tend to eat poorly (eating interferes with drinking time), don't exercise and are liable to smoke, and live generally unhealthy lives.

Some research (quoted in *Painful Affairs*) suggests that the combined effect of cigarettes and alcohol has more than twice the ageing effect of either habit indulged in singly.

The human body is a highly adaptive organism

and can learn to tolerate alcohol up to a point but, when alcohol is taken on a regular basis, the body learns to 'expect' it and withdrawal symptoms can set in when it is not present. This also puts a severe strain on body systems. Alcohol intake on a massive scale affects the immune system, so that infections of all kinds are more common, last longer and are more difficult to treat than in someone whose body remains relatively free of the substance.

Q A lot of people use alcohol to help relieve stress. Does this work?

Yes, up to a point. Because alcohol is a powerful depressant drug, it can act as a highly effective tranquillizer, drowning sorrows and instilling a mood of spurious optimism. People often drink precisely for this effect. The problem for most people is that a single drink is not enough to produce this effect and more drinks start to make them drunk. Sufferers from acute or chronic stress may start to rely on drink as a means of relief, and may become alcoholics as a result.

In any case, the stress-relieving effect is extremely short-lived and will, eventually, have the opposite effect to the one intended.

Regular heavy drinking can actually increase stress

and this returns tenfold when there is no alcohol in the system. For problem drinkers, nervousness also increases without alcohol, the danger being that the drinker is tempted to consume ever-increasing amounts in order to overcome stress and tension. Eventually they are not only left with the initial stress, which remains unresolved, but also have the additional stress that comes from being a problem drinker.

Therefore, using drink to solve a problem only results in the problem eventually being multiplied. Drink does not make stress go away because it does not reach the cause of the stress and address it.

Q Does alcohol make you put on weight?

Alcoholic drinks, because of their high sugar content, are all extremely high in calories. The calorie contents of the following are:

Stout, bottled (568 ml/1 UK pt)   200
Medium wine, one glass
    (125 ml/approx. ¼ UK pt)   105
Gin, (25 ml/approx. ⅙ UK gill) and
    tonic (113 ml/approx. ⅕ UK pt)   80
Whisky (25ml/approx. ¹⁄₁₆ UK gill)   60

Some alcoholics grow fat and others become thin. The fat ones are eating huge amounts of food, often of low nutritional value, in addition to their alcohol consumption, whereas the thin ones are probably using alcohol as a substitute for food.

In addition, alcohol can prevent the body absorbing and utilizing vitamins, especially those of the B and C groups, which are essential for body maintenance and resistance to infection. Indeed, vitamin deficiency may be a sign of alcohol abuse.

Q How does alcohol affect specific body systems?

The main organ eventually affected by alcohol is the liver, as this has to work hard to detoxify the alcohol which is continually being consumed. Although the liver is a very tough organ, in time it may not be able to cope and therefore becomes scarred. This is due to acetaldehyde formation and is known as *cirrhosis of the liver*, a condition found mainly in alcohol abusers and one which means that progressively less of the liver is functional.

Q What about alcohol and pregnancy?

In the USA, fears about alcohol damaging the unborn baby have become so rife that pregnant women are advised not to drink any alcohol at all. In fact, moderate drinking – 6 units or less a week – is unlikely to damage the unborn baby, especially if the drinks are taken at long intervals. Foetal Alcohol Syndrome, which results in physical and mental retardation and characteristic facial features, is in fact very rare. Nevertheless, it is wise for women who are pregnant, or trying to get pregnant, not to drink more than a few glasses on any one occasion.

There are other reasons, however, why it is not a good idea to drink more than a glass or two of wine a day during pregnancy. As we have seen, alcohol consumption tends to leach valuable vitamins and minerals out of the system and even quite small amounts can make people unsteady on their feet.

Breast-feeding women were once advised to drink a glass of stout a day. This is no longer the case but, again, it is unlikely that moderate drinking of the kind recommended during pregnancy will do any harm to the baby.

The worst dangers of overconsumption as far as children are concerned are not the effects on the drinker's health, but the ways in which it can adversely affect adult behaviour and family relationships.

Q Is it easy to diagnose alcoholism by physical signs?

Those working with people suffering from drinking problems would say definitely yes. There are giveaway signs in the teeth, jaws and skin. Gingivitis, poor dental hygiene and bad teeth are generally present and the skin may show blemishes, slow wound healing, bruises, scratches, cuts and premature ageing.

There may also be more generalized body changes. There is often an appearance of bloating – the 'beer belly' – or of excessive thinness.

In later stages, there may be high blood pressure (hypertension), hepatitis and insomnia. In fact, insomnia is a serious problem connected with alcohol abuse, as alcohol severely disrupts sleeping patterns.

But, of course, there are many people who drink too much, who show no such physical signs.

Q What about high blood pressure?

Most alcoholics and chronic alcohol-abusers will eventually develop high blood pressure. But you do not have to be a problem drinker for alcohol to have this effect. The 1992 Health Survey for

England interviewed 4,000 adults and found that men drinking over 21 units a week (the current recommended level) were 25 per cent more likely than others to have raised blood pressure. But the picture is complicated because high blood pressure is also associated with stress, and people under stress often over-use alcohol.

Raised blood pressure is also associated with increasing age, obesity and certain medical treatments, so a straight forward link with moderate alcohol consumption is rather difficult to establish.

Excessive alcohol consumption – say 50 units a week or more – will almost always cause high blood pressure.

 Can alcohol cause cancer?

In 1988 the International Agency for Research on Cancer concluded, after sifting through over 1,000 research papers on the subject, that alcoholic beverages were carcinogenic (cancer-causing) to human beings. There is some evidence that excessive alcohol consumption can lead to cancer by means of either the indirect effect of acetaldehyde (produced by alcohol metabolism) or the effect of non-alcoholic substances in the beverages.

According to the British Medical Journal (1994), the

incidence of throat, liver, stomach and bowel cancers have all been linked to excessive alcohol consumption and some research suggests that consumption of two to three drinks a day is associated with an increased risk of breast cancer for women. However, at this stage of research, there is insufficient hard evidence for a causal relationship to be made between breast cancer and alcohol consumption.

Q Does alcohol destroy brain cells?

It has been said that alcohol progressively destroys the frontal lobes of the brain, eventually making the alcoholic, quite literally, lobotomized. It is in the frontal lobes that moral and ethical judgements are thought to be made and perspectives clouded. Certainly, alcoholics often appear to be excessively obstinate and unreasonable, and unable to see what is causing their problem.

However, some Danish research has now questioned this and suggests that any such damage may be reversible. A comparative study of the brains of dead chronic alcoholics and normal men found no differences (British Medical Journal, 1994).

As alcoholism progresses, however, memory loss becomes irreversible as neurons are destroyed, and the memory centres are never restored. Other brain matter, however, will regenerate itself if drinking is stopped.

Q Are there any other health dangers?

In some people, alcohol abuse can cause a particular type of hand deformity known as *Dupuytren's Contracture*, in which the palms of the hands become thickened and wrinkled, and the fingers contract permanently.

Heavy drinking over a number of years can also lead to a condition known as cardiomyopathy or – 'beer-drinker's heart', which is a weakening of the heart muscle.

Q Are any other important organs damaged by alcohol abuse?

The pancreas is affected in a similar way to the liver and becomes inflamed when too much alcohol is taken into the system. This has the effect of interfering with the production of certain digestive enzymes so that alcoholics are unable to absorb food properly from the intestines. Acute pancreatitis can be fatal.

Alcohol thus interferes with effective nutrition, and so alcoholics are generally malnourished. Apart from the fact that they are mostly not eating a good diet, the adverse changes in their digestive organs mean that nutrients are neither digested nor absorbed properly.

Vitamin deficiency is a common feature of alcoholism and most alcoholics are deficient in essential vitamins. This can eventually lead to severe organ and tissue damage.

Thiamine deficiency, for example can lead to a condition known as *Wernicke's Encephalopathy*, the symptoms of which are total confusion, difficulty in focusing the eyes and difficulty in walking. Other vitamin and mineral deficiencies can lead to muscle weakness, pain, diminished sensation to touch, and strange, frightening sensations coming from the extremities.

Q What exactly are the DTs (delirium tremens)?

Delirium tremens is a serious, acute psychotic condition caused only by chronic alcohol abuse. It is a state of profound confusion and the sufferer experiences hallucinations – seeing, smelling, hearing or feeling things which do not, in fact, exist. There are also physical signs, such as raised temperature and pulse rate, profuse sweating and tremors which shake the whole body.

Symptoms usually set in 2–3 days after a severe drinking bout. In the old days, death from the DTs was not uncommon and occurred in 25 per cent of alcoholism cases. Today, with earlier diagnosis and the availability of skilled medical care, death from the DTs is far less common.

Q What is the 'holiday heart syndrome'?

This is a serious condition, caused by excessive and uncontrolled 'binge-drinking', i.e. consumption of large quantities of alcohol in one session. The term was originally coined because these drinking episodes often occur during holiday celebrations.

Irregularities in heart beat, e.g. premature beats and double beats, are a feature of this condition. The patient feels dizzy, faint and weak and, if taken to hospital, may well be diagnosed as alcoholic. If the alcoholism has not progressed to the very severe stages, the only malfunction may be a disturbance in the rhythm of the heart beat.

Q I have heard it said that alcohol can have a similar effect to having a stroke. Is this true?

Yes. The symptoms of alcohol intoxication have many things in common with those of a stroke.

These are: slowed and thick speech, failure to make eye contact, frustration in communicating, repetitive behaviour and temporary or permanent brain damage.

Q What about the good aspects of alcohol? Are there any?

Alcohol is, of course, one of the oldest medicines known because of its pronounced anaesthetic effects. In the days when surgical operations were performed without anaesthetic, alcohol was often given to dull the pain.

A growing number of doctors now believe that two glasses of red wine a day can have a protective effect on the heart, but that more than this, on a regular basis, can have the opposite effect, and vastly increase the risk of heart attacks and coronary heart disease.

The late Dr E. Maury, a French homeopathic doctor, believed that extra dry champagne could improve digestion, help to fight bacterial infections, prevent hardening of the arteries, increase metabolism and help to boost the immune system, but there is no particular evidence to support this idea.

Dr Maury also believed that most alcoholic ills were caused by drinking on an empty stomach and said that the best way to enjoy wine was with a meal. At the very least, snacks, such as peanuts or crisps, should always be taken with wine to slow down the rate of absorption of alcohol from the gut. Another feature of Dr Maury's philosophy was that good wines were far healthier than commercially concocted fizzy drinks.

A British Regional Heart Study showed that people consuming six drinks a day were *as* healthy as abstainers, although few of them were actually healthier.

Q Is there any research to show that people who abstain completely are far healthier in every way than drinkers?

No, not conclusively. Research in the USA, carried out among such groups as Mormons and Seventh-Day Adventists, both fundamentalist Christian groups which do not touch any alcohol at all, had far fewer cases of· serious illness, such as cancer and heart disease, than other sections of the population.

However, what the research does not reveal is how much of this effect is due to their eating and drinking patterns, and how much to having a definite sense of purpose and spiritual goal in life.

Some British studies have showed total abstainers to be more unhealthy than moderate drinkers; However, some of these teetotallers were found to be former alcoholics who had 'dried out'. It is true that total abstainers are more likely to suffer heart disease than light drinkers, but they are no more at risk from any other illness. About 10 per cent of the population in the West are in fact total abstainers. This includes, among others, people belonging to strict religious groups and dried-out alcoholics.

At the moment, then, the picture is clouded, and no research so far has showed us what effect personality has on serious illnesses. But certainly any man drinking less than half a bottle of wine a day on average (slightly less for a woman) probably has no need to worry about alcohol intake adversely affecting health. It is drinking on a massive scale which does the physical harm.

However, it is worth remembering that many people will suffer social harm because of their actions when intoxicated, e.g. driving accidents, and these people may not be chronic excessive drinkers.

3 Alcoholism Explained

Q **When most people seem to be able to drink within reasonable limits, why is it that some people seem unable to control their drinking?**

Nobody knows for sure, although a great deal of research has now taken place on this. Noble and Blum (*Journal of the American Medical Association*, 1990) believe that certain people have a 'gene', or predisposition, for alcohol addiction and that the first drink will trigger off such a craving that alcoholism rapidly develops. Not everyone has this gene and, in any case, there is still great argument about its existence.

Although we may never discover exactly whether there is a physical cause for alcoholism, one thing seems certain: alcoholics often drink with the express purpose of arriving at oblivion. They drink to change their personalities; they drink because alcohol is a close friend with a guaranteed effect; they drink because alcohol is addictive. Over many years, they take ever-increasing amounts of alcohol; indeed, some alcoholics can drink amounts which would kill anyone who was not addicted.

It seems that some personalities are more liable to

become alcoholics than others. Professor Hans Eysenck, the psychologist who developed the introvert-extrovert personality scale, believes that alcohol abuse is associated with an extrovert personality, and with lack of inhibition and repression.

At the moment, however, nobody knows what leads one extrovert to drink to excess while another can keep his or her drinking within tolerable limits.

Q What is the difference between alcohol use and abuse?

People who 'use' alcohol, as opposed to abusing it, do so in order to improve their social lives, enhance their meals or enjoy parties more. Such people are able to alternate alcoholic with non-alcoholic drinks and savour the wines or other drinks they are taking.

For those who abuse alcohol, alcoholic drink becomes a focus in their lives rather than an occasional pleasure. Serious drinkers may fit into the following pattern. These people may not really care what they drink, as long as it is alcoholic, and as long as there is enough of it. They may prefer spirits to other drinks because the effect is quicker and they may also neglect to eat well because drinking and getting drunk are far more important.

However, it is a mistake to assume that this is the pattern followed by all alcoholics. Some people with serious addiction may have favourite types of alcoholic drink, may savour and be knowledgeable about wines and may also have an appreciation of good food and eat well. Some alcoholics may continually top up so that they maintain a level of alcohol in their bloodstream, but at the same time may never appear to be drunk.

Q Are there any other reasons why people might drink too much?

A Swedish test, known as the Alcohol Expectancy Questionnaire, lists 68 items representing the possible effects of drinking. At the top is pleasure – both physical and social. It seems that, for some people, alcohol activates a 'pleasure gene', but these, of course, are not the people who become alcoholics. Alcoholics drink not for pleasure but solely to alter their mood, behaviour and perceptions.

Q How do I know if I, or somebody close to me, is becoming dependent on drink?

The Alcohol Use Disorders Identification Test

(AUDIT) is a 10-item questionnaire, developed by the World Health Organisation in collaboration with six countries, and designed to identify those at an early stage of risk.

The questions are:

1. How often do you have a drink containing alcohol?

2. How many drinks containing alcohol do you have on a typical day when drinking?

3. How often do you have six or more drinks on one occasion?

4. How often during the last year have you found you were not able to stop drinking once you had started?

5. How often during the last year have you failed to do what was normally expected of you because of drinking?

6. How often during the last year have you needed a first drink in the morning to get yourself going after a heavy drinking session?

7. How often during the last year have you had a feeling of guilt or remorse after drinking?

8. How often during the last year have you been unable to remember what happened the night before because you had been drinking?

9. Have you or someone else been injured as a result of your drinking?

10. Has a relative or friend or doctor or other health worker been concerned about your drinking or suggested you cut down?

The scoring procedure is as follows:
Questions 1–8 are scored 0, 1, 2, 3 or 4.
Questions 9 and 10 are scored 0, 2 or 4 only.
The response coding is as follows:

	Question 1	Question 2	Question 3–8	Question 9–10
0	Never	1 or 2	Never	No
1	Monthly or less	3 or 4	Less than monthly	
2	Two to four times per month	5 or 6	Monthly	Yes, but not in the last year
3	Two to three times per week	7 to 9	Weekly	
4	Four or more times per week	10 or more	Daily or almost daily	Yes, during the last year

The minimum score (for non-drinkers) is 0 and the maximum possible score is 40. A score of 8 or more indicates a strong likelihood of hazardous or harmful alcohol consumption.

Routine screening with readily-used and scored instruments such as this might have some impact upon subsequent alcohol-related problems for there is good evidence that it is often sufficient for a potential problem drinker to merely go through an assessment procedure to be diverted away from future harm.

Q **Is there some simple test you can take which determines whether you're drinking too much?**

No. Although several tests exist, including the Gamma GT which tests liver function, all will produce false positives and false negatives, and cannot be relied on. The only real 'test', is whether the drinking is doing any harm or might lead to harm.

Q **Do alcoholics drink every single day?**

Not necessarily. This is one of the misconceptions made by non-alcoholics. Another is that alcoholics always drink in the morning. Some alcoholics drink steadily and continuously while others go for days, perhaps months, without having a drink then consume large amounts at one session. This 'binge drinking' is an overwhelming characteristic of an alcoholic. When it does occur, it is always uncontrolled.

Why are some people unable to control their drinking?

This is very difficult for non-alcoholics to understand as most people feel ill when they drink too much. Although many young people drink to excess, this is very often a passing phase, a rite of passage, which will not lead to alcoholism in later life. Doctors often advise their patients not to drink so much and are annoyed when they cannot do so. But the thing to understand about the nature of any addiction is that it controls you.

It seems likely that, in some way, certain people find that they and alcohol 'fit each other' from the very first gulp. Others start drinking for a variety of reasons, perhaps social, and then find that they cannot control their intake.

The American expert on addiction, Dr Joseph Cruse, author of *Painful Affairs*, a book about his own alcoholism, believes it is very much like a love affair. You fall in love with drink because it provides the relief you have been searching for since birth, and a wonderful feeling floods over you. You arrive, through alcohol, at a feeling which has so far eluded you and you want to experience that feeling time and again.

Alcoholism develops because, as time goes on,

ever larger quantities are needed to gain this effect and, eventually, alcohol has to be taken just to feel normal. Also, because alcohol is addictive, it means that the body in time starts to require and demand it.

One view suggests that people who do not become problem drinkers do not share this attitude towards drink. For them, the first alcoholic drink is often distasteful and, although they may get drunk on occasion, they do not rush headlong into a lifelong love affair with the intoxicating liquor.

Q Why is alcohol so hard to give up?

Two explanations for this have been put forward: chemical dependency, which eventually affects all body systems, and the fact that alcoholics have built their lives around drinking for so long that they cannot imagine living without it. They don't just drink uncontrollably – they have joined a drinking way of life which seems impossible to give up. All their social life centres around alcohol; all their friends are drinkers. The question is: what do you replace all this with? Whatever could mean as much?

The other thing is that, eventually, an alcoholic's whole life becomes centred around the next drink.

But we also have to take into account the sheer force of habit, when people have simply become accustomed to drinking certain amounts each day.

Q How does alcoholism develop?

Alcoholism may be divided into four stages: early, middle, crucial and chronic. These categories can be useful in helping to identify whether someone has an alcohol problem and in assessing how serious it is. However, it is a simplistic model and many alcoholics do not follow this progression. Although most alcohol-related problems start with social drinking it is not a certainty that problem drinking will inevitably lead to the symptoms described here as chronic. Many people reach a potentially harmful level of dependence on alcohol without displaying the behaviour described here as crucial or chronic.

The early stage is characterized by what most people would probably term 'social drinking'. An alcoholic eventually crosses that line when drinking is no longer purely social but starts to assume an ever-greater importance in his or her life. Other people, even their nearest and dearest, become secondary to the drink.

At the early stage of problem drinking, alcoholics may exhibit noticeable changes in behaviour, and anger at people or situations which get in the way of their drinking. They react aggressively when others question the amounts that they are drinking.

It is at this point that the second stage is reached. There is now a marked dependence on alcohol and an urgent need for a drink. They may now start to take risks with alcohol, such as driving when over the limit, or working under the influence of alcohol, and they feel remorse or guilt about their drinking.

They may start to lie about their alcohol use and deny it. They may plan drinking binges and start to have problems remembering while drunk. There will also be noticeable mood swings.

This brings us to the crucial stage, when the alcoholic is unable to control the amount of alcohol he or she consumes, and drinks to excess on every drinking occasion. They make promises which are quickly broken and behaviour worsens. There will now be frequent tantrums, unrealistic resentments and personal hygiene starts to suffer. Eating is a distraction from drinking and so they become chronically undernourished.

Alcoholics who drink daily feel sick in the morning, possibly vomiting. They have tremors and their hands shake. They may not even be able to write their name at times. They have to drink in order to be able to face the day and they always drink to help themselves cope with routine situations. Eventually, they are in a permanent state of intoxication.

The final, and chronic, stage is reached when they become obsessed with drinking to the exclusion of everything else. They have lost touch with their feelings and no longer have any sense of self.

They abandon all responsibility for themselves, their families and their work. They have frequent accidents and suffer from worsening health. They begin to be financially dishonest and memory blackouts increase. Life has become a complete pre-occupation with alcohol, to the point where nothing else matters.

Q Is the problem worse for men or for women?

Alcoholism is a progressive disease that follows the same course in both men and women, except that for women there are two added dangers: pregnancy and sex.

As inhibitions are removed and the search for alcohol and oblivion becomes ever more marked, there is increased carelessness about sexual relationships. This, in some ways, is less of a danger for men, as few men can get an erection when drunk and prolonged alcohol use leads to impotence.

For women, there is no such protection. A woman under the influence can always be sexually used – she just has not to resist. Also, when under the chronic influence of alcohol, women seem to become 'sexier' and more available, and to seek out sexual gratification more. This entails the risk of unwanted pregnancy, of diseases associated with promiscuous sex, and, if pregnancy results, of producing a child with Foetal Alcohol Syndrome (see page 32). A great number of women with a drink problem turn to prostitution to pay for their habit – alcoholism is a very expensive disease, or at least becomes so eventually.

Q Why do alcoholics so often blame other people for their drinking?

One of the major problems of alcohol addiction is that sufferers cease to take responsibility for themselves or their actions. This has nothing to do with their intelligence or acute perception in other areas of life. Also, few people want to admit, either to themselves or to others, that they cannot control their behaviour, so the easiest course of action is to blame others. This is very childish but alcoholics can be childish. The disease makes people behave irresponsibly, even when they are highly intelligent.

Q Does easy access to alcohol make the problem worse?

It seems to be the case that in all countries where alcohol consumption goes up, alcohol-related problems also rise. In cultures which do not drink alcohol, such as the Arabic-Islamic countries, other drugs are taken instead. Of course, if there is no alcohol at all, and no way of making it, then nobody could become an alcoholic.

But Prohibition in the USA, in which alcohol became illegal, did not stem the tide of alcoholism. Indeed, in some ways it made the problem worse because all alcohol had to be made illegally and, as there was no quality control, many people became ill, or even died, as a result of contaminated liquor. Eventually, Prohibition itself had to be abolished because it was found to be having the opposite effect to the one intended.

It is true to say that, today, in countries where alcohol is harder or more expensive to obtain the problem of alcoholism still exists.

The West these days is definitely a drinking culture with increasing amounts of wine and other alcoholic beverages being manufactured and sold all the time. In the US, certain states have changed their legislation over the years with the result that alcohol has become more easily available to the public. In Idaho and Maine in the early 1970s, for example, more outlets – like grocery stores – were licensed to sell wine. Legislation in North Carolina in 1975 relaxed to permit the sale of distilled spirits in public establishments. Other states have brought in similar relaxation of the laws.

This has provided an opportunity for studies to be carried out to assess whether increased availability has had any effect on drinking habits and alcohol-related problems. The results have not, as yet, been sufficiently conclusive for any hard-and-fast judgements to be made. It is interesting to note that although wine-drinking has increased dramatically over the past 30 years, beer-drinking has stayed the same.

What we can say for certain is that alcoholism has never been a marginal problem in Western society but is, in fact, very common. There is probably hardly a family in the UK which has not, at one time, contained at least one alcoholic, and people who have managed to trace back their families through generations have nearly always discovered an alcoholic somewhere along the line.

Q Are there some alcoholic drinks more likely to induce addiction than others?

No, not really. Although some drinks contain far more alcohol than others, alcoholics will drink anything which has the magical effect. In time, beer and wine become too slow-acting and spirits will be resorted to, but alcoholics may drink anything containing alcohol – even cough mixture – rather than nothing at all.

Q Do alcoholics usually have problems with other addictions, such as smoking, gambling or drug taking?

Often, yes. All treatment centres which take the problem seriously have found that nearly all alcoholics have problems related to other substances. Most of them smoke, the vast majority gamble, and a considerable majority are womanizers or sexually promiscuous.

One problem, as many workers in the field have noted, is that alcoholics are often extremely nice people: amusing, talented, creative and original. This often leads others mistakenly to believe that drink and a dissolute way of life somehow enhances creativity and talent. When in fact, it progressively destroys it.

Q How long does it take for a problem drinker to become an alcoholic?

For many people the average length of time between the first drink and serious alcoholism is 20 years; but dedicated alcoholics may become hopelessly addicted in far less time. On the other hand a few people manage to drink excessively for far longer before suffering serious damage.

Q Does alcoholism run in families?

Yes, definitely. Again, we do not know exactly why, or whether this is due to nature or nurture, but research seems to indicate that addicts breed addicts (*Journal of the American Medical Association*, 1985). They are attracted to addicts, they marry and form relationships with other addicts, and the children copy their parents. In some cases, there may be a genetic element, but not always.

It is of course completely possible for a person to develop alcoholism quite out of the blue and for the pattern not to be repeated. But this is not the usual course of events and the dysfunction tends to run from generation to generation.

One might imagine that children, having seen their parents drink, and having witnessed the devastation it can cause, would instantly sign the pledge and swear never to touch a drop. In fact, the opposite seems to happen, perhaps because, in such families, drinking, violence, abuse and all the associated problems are eventually viewed as normal.

This highly complicated issue, the subject of literally thousands of books in the USA, has led to the formation of the Association for the Children of Alcoholics (ACOA). One of the biggest problems surrounding alcohol abuse within the family is that it is often strenuously denied by all family members – including the active alcoholic.

The problem has been likened to having an elephant in the living room and everybody walking round it, not admitting it is there. In families where alcohol is abused, every effort is made to appear normal, and like everybody else.

Q Why is the problem so fiercely denied?

Well, would you want people to know you were an alcoholic and not able to control your drinking? For many years, centuries even, uncontrolled drinking was seen as shameful, a moral weakness. The stigma attached to alcoholism has still not completely disappeared because there still remains a lingering idea that people ought to be able to control what they drink.

There are also social factors, particularly at work: those known to have a drink problem may face dismissal or be considered incompetent. The wonder is that so many alcoholics can carry on work for so long, with nobody but them suspecting the truth.

Dr Joseph Cruse, a recovered alcoholic, recalls in his book *Painful Affairs* that he treated patients while drunk, diagnosed illnesses while drunk, and carried on his work as a very successful doctor. Many alcoholics, he says, are people who appear to be pillars of the community, and it would not do for their secret to get out.

The primary symptom of alcoholism is the person's own denial of the reality of the situation. Instead of giving up drink, the alcoholic tries to devise ways of changing drinking patterns to make the addiction seem more accessible, more within limits. Dr Cruse admits in his book that he never saw himself as an alcoholic at all – simply as a naughty little boy – when he was hiding bottles in his sports jacket – or in his doctor's bag.

He could not let himself see it any other way because it would have been too painful. Most alcoholics go through this pattern of thinking, justifying, hiding, deluding.

Q Is there such a thing as an alcoholic personality?

There may be. There seem to be certain characteristics which are common to a lot of active alcoholics, namely: impulsiveness, inability to delay gratification, dislike of strong feelings, a propensity for panic-level anxiety and prolonged depression, and an unclear, confused, sense of identity.

In addition, most alcoholics are also 'co-dependent', an American term, allied to addiction, whereby the sufferer relies on substances or activities outside himself or herself to gain a sense of self-worth and identity. Nevertheless, many people who become alcoholic are extremely gifted, creative, sensitive and perceptive people.

Q Can alcohol make people more creative?

Some creative people seem able to express themselves only after loosening their inhibitions with alcohol, but alcohol cannot make a creative genius out of just anyone.

This belief has come about because many highly gifted people, indeed geniuses, have been alcoholic. Also, many alcoholic poets and playwrights have written movingly about alcohol. The wonder, in the case of many alcoholic geniuses, is that they were able to create anything at all, considering the amount they drank, or that their brains continued to function at any meaningful level.

Q It is often said that all alcoholics eventually become indistinguishable from one another. Is it true and if so, why?

Yes, this is partly true. This is because, as alcoholism proceeds, all that sufferers can eventually do is to stumble towards the next drink. Also, as alcohol eventually affects all brain systems and perceptions so profoundly, alcoholics' characters become alike – devious, childish, irresponsible and self-pitying. In sober moments, there is also self-loathing, but this is coupled with a propensity to blame others, rather than themselves, for their predicament.

Q What are the standard behaviour patterns of an alcoholic?

David Stafford, Director of the St Joseph's Centre for Addiction in Surrey, UK, believes that all alcoholics exhibit the following tendencies: in his book, *Children of Alcoholics*, he says:

They deny the problem and blame others. They

forget, and tell stories to defend themselves against attack and criticism. They become unpredictable and impulsive in behaviour. They resort to physical and verbal abuse instead of reasonable talk. They lose the trust of family and friends. There is no longer any interest in sex. There are increasing feelings of despair and hopelessness, and there may well be a suicide attempt. There is also considerable deterioration of physical health.

Q Can alcoholism itself be considered a disease?

Many people now believe that alcoholism is a progressive disease, like diabetes or short-sightedness. In other words, it is something that the individual cannot help, and cannot cure, but can control or overcome. Some current alcoholism experts consider that people who become alcoholic are those whose bodies and systems simply cannot handle alcoholic beverages.

There are, though, many other experts who believe that people drink excessively for understandable reasons, and that they can unlearn this behaviour with practice, just as they learned it to start with. Some serious drinkers will be helped by one approach, and some by another. It doesn't matter which – so long as it works.

Q How does the family deal with these problems?

In some cases, the alcoholic will be thrown out of his home but, more usually, the problem is denied for as long as possible. The coping strategies of family members include marking or hiding bottles, refusing to buy alcohol and avoiding the alcoholic – all of which isolate the alcoholic still further. There may also be nagging, threats and attempts to get the alcoholic to change his behaviour and his drinking habits.

Needless to say, the strategies never work because alcoholics are, above all, experts at making others feel responsible and guilty for their own behaviour. A typical response is: 'I'd be all right if only you stopped going on at me.'

Many alcoholics eventually lose their moral and ethical standards, and may lie, cheat, resort to prostitution, criminal practices or sexual and physical abuse – all behaviours which they would find appalling when sober and in command of their faculties.

Q Why do alcoholics go on drinking when they have reached this stage?

Quite simply, because they cannot stop. Alcoholics

continue to drink, even when mental and physical deterioration have reached an advanced stage, because they know that they will experience unpleasant withdrawal symptoms if they stop. In the early stages of abstinence alcoholics feel worse than when they were drinking – just as smokers feel terrible when they try to give up cigarettes. Denial of the problem eventually appears to be the easiest way to carry on living.

Also, an alcoholic at least knows what to expect if he continues to drink. He has no idea, or has forgotten, what life might be like on the other, abstinent, side.

Many have become unable to comprehend that they are in any way responsible for what has happened to them, and they persist in their grandiose behaviour. In fact, this very grandiosity is a sign of severe alcoholism.

Q Is there a standard, or average, amount for an alcoholic to drink per day?

No. People can be seriously addicted to alcohol, and be doing themselves and others serious harm, at fairly moderate intakes. At the extreme, though, many people manage to drink two bottles of spirits each and every day.

Q Is it possible to abuse alcohol without actually being alcoholic?

Yes, it is. Some people abuse alcohol without really understanding what it can do and how harmful it can be. Usually, for these people, a terrifying incident, such as a car accident while drunk, violence, or a skirmish with the law will be enough to stop them drinking so much in the future. An alcoholic cannot moderate his drinking, however hard he tries.

Q Are alcoholics more likely than others to take prescription or over-the-counter drugs?

Yes, it seems that alcoholics will take anything that they can get hold of. Alcoholics are dedicated users of over-the-counter medicines, such as antacids, as they frequently suffer from peptic ulcers. They also often use anti-depressants and tranquillizers and are frequently admitted to hospital. Alcoholism – often apparent by the level of liver damage – is sometimes, but rarely diagnosed when the drinker is hospitalized for some other cause.

Q Can alcoholics ever form good relationships with other people?

Alcoholics are often popular because many are extrovert, witty and generous. But when it comes to close or intimate relationships they often have severe difficulties. When somebody drinks to excess, they are, in effect, saying that they are damping down their real feelings. It is possible that these feelings were damped down or denied before heavy consumption started, but drinking to excess confirms this.

According to Lynn Buess, author of *Children of Light, Children of Denial*, alcohol is basically a self-chosen form of anaesthesia. It means that you do not have to feel.

Because of this, it is difficult for alcoholics to communicate their feelings to their partner. Therefore, the partner shuts down as well and, before long, all real communication ceases and the relationship degenerates into one where the most important thing is dealing with the drink.

In place of honesty, spontaneity, intimacy and genuine rapport, there will be games, manipulation, lies, hostility, coldness, blame. If there are children of this relationship, they will learn to shut down their feelings as well, so that no one is properly relating to anyone else. It is a hollow sham. The children, in turn, learn to lie, be manipulative, secretive, judgemental. Then, as these children grow up, they are all too liable to repeat the pattern.

4 Recovery from Alcoholism

Q **If this physical and moral decline is so serious and so inevitable, what motivates anybody to try and recover?**

The usual answer given is that, when alcoholics have reached their own personal 'rock bottom', they will try to turn the tide. For some, this could be loss of a job; for others, loss of a relationship. For many, it will be a suicide attempt, loss of consciousness or a serious accident closely related to their alcoholism. The only crucial factor in recovery is a fervent wish to be sober.

Q **Can other people persuade the alcoholic to recover?**

Not usually. Because alcoholics have become impervious to reason, and their reasoning powers are seriously disturbed anyway, they will usually fend off all attempts to help by others as busybodying and interfering. In almost all cases, alcoholics can recover only when, for their own personal reasons, they themselves have made the decision to do so.

Q Can people ever recover from serious alcoholism on their own?

They may do so but, by the time the chronic stage has been reached, this is very difficult, as chemical dependency has been established for many years and the body has come to rely on alcohol. The good news is that people have recovered from all stages of alcoholism, even the chronic one. But usually they need help from experts and may also require treatment in a hospital detoxification unit.

The other good news is that the body has marvellous powers of self-recovery and, if alcohol abuse ceases, it will regenerate itself to a remarkable extent. Even if body organs have been abused for too long for full recovery to be a possibility, there will always be some degree of regeneration.

The main problem for alcoholics, as with all drug users, is not so much the physical withdrawal – although this can be unpleasant in the extreme – as release from the way of life that goes with it. Most alcoholics wonder whatever they can do to replace their addiction to alcohol when their whole existence has become centred around drinking.

Q What happens during withdrawal?

If you, or a family member or friend, have been

drinking way over safe limits for years, it may be best to withdraw, or detoxify, within a hospital unit. In the UK, and USA there are many of these such units, both National Health Service (in the UK) and private, where detoxification is carried out under skilled medical supervision.

Withdrawal symptoms usually start 3 to 6 hours after the last drink and usually last between 5 and 7 days. Early symptoms – up to 12 hours after the last drink – include tremor, sweating, loss of appetite, nausea, insomnia, anxiety. These may be highly unpleasant and hallucinations may occur.

Between 10 and 16 hours after the last drink there may be a risk of seizures and these either precede or accompany delirium tremens (DTs). After 72 hours, a few people may develop the DTs with severe tremors, confusion, disorientation, agitation, visual and auditory hallucinations and paranoia. About 5 per cent of alcoholics admitted to hospital develop the DTs, so it is not as common as popularly believed. The older the person who is detoxifying, the greater the risk of problems developing.

In-patient management consists of reassurance and good nursing care plus rehydration. In some cases, sedative drugs and anti-anxiety drugs (anxiolytics) may be given.

Q **How do private detoxification centres vary from hospital ones?**

Private centres treating alcoholism usually offer group therapy, counselling, nutrition advice and one-to-one therapy in addition to the physical detoxification. The usual length of stay is 4 to 6 weeks, and fees are high.

Most private treatment centres are based on the Minnesota Model (see page 87) and have a very high staff-to-patient ratio. Rooms are comfortable and facilities are usually luxurious, but the regime is strict and must be adhered to. The punishment for disobeying instructions, drinking or not turning up for therapy sessions is instant dismissal. As one counsellor working in a detoxification unit said: 'This is the only prison where you are turned out for bad behaviour'.

Hospital detox. units can successfully detoxify the alcoholic, but most do not – or cannot – offer the kind of intensive therapy offered at the private units. However, doctors and psychiatrists are becoming more sympathetic to alcohol-abusers, and certain types of therapy, or models of approach, may be offered. Hospital detox. units vary a lot, depending on the facilities available

Q Can my doctor refer me to a detox. unit?

Yes, certainly, although many people do not like to admit to their doctor that they have an alcohol problem. Also, very few doctors in general practice are experts in alcohol-related problems. You can self-refer if you like. Many alcoholics agree to be referred to a detox. unit /when they have had a serious accident or illness caused directly by alcohol – and have frightened themselves badly. Others may decide to go to a detox. unit when they have had a confrontation with the police or been taken to court.

Very often, it takes something drastic to bring about the decision to do something about the drinking problem.

Q I have heard of Alcoholics Anonymous, but what is it, and why does it have to be anonymous?

The principle behind Alcoholics Anonymous, or AA as it is usually known, is based on the belief that alcoholism above all, is a disease of the spirit. It was started by two alcoholics in 1935 on the basis that those who become alcoholic have somehow become separated from their true selves and that alcohol use is an attempt, albeit dysfunctional, to merge the alienated self with the real self.

Although AA accepts that alcohol has very definite physical effects on the body and the brain, it operates by concentrating on character and seeks to replace selfishness, and lack of responsibility and care for others with honesty, humility and patience. The idea is that, by developing spirituality, permanent sobriety can be achieved, and the appeal is to a Higher Power.

Through AA meetings, alcoholics come to a new understanding of themselves as spiritual beings, where they are prepared to make changes, be open-minded and confess their sins. Some people have objected to what they see as the religious flavour to AA but, in its favour, it must be said that it can, and does, work for many people.

The AA philosophy is that uncontrolled and excessive alcoholic drinking – where the aim is always oblivion – is a dysfunctional reflection of the deep human need for spiritual life and growth. This is one reason why alcoholics are very often deeply sensitive and spiritual people, and often very gifted and perceptive.

The goal at AA is complete abstinence, sobriety for ever. AA does not believe that an alcoholic can ever become a controlled drinker, although some other treatment models believe that moderate drinking can eventually be resumed.

The idea of anonymity is partly to protect those who do not want their identities known, and partly because each alcoholic is seen to be like every other alcoholic. There is no need for identification, other than through first names, as the only thing members need know about each other is that they are all in the same boat.

Meetings consist of confessions, stories, inspiration and self-searching. The underlying philosophy is that the power of the group is far greater than any that an individual can summon up alone. All addictions isolate the addicts, and so AA meetings provide solace and comfort for those who thought they were the only ones with their particular problem. AA tries to help its members find a new meaning in their lives.

Very often, people are recommended to go to AA meetings after they have detoxified in hospital.

Q How does AA work?

AA is basically a self-help organization, with branches all over the world, where alcoholics are their own experts. Any AA meeting will consist of members who are in various stages of recovery. One of the most famous tenets of the AA philosophy is that recovery is taken 'one day at a time'. Members pledge that 'just for today' they will not drink, though backsliding is of course extremely common.

At all meetings, the so-called 'Twelve Steps' will be discussed and repeated. The root of AA's philosophy is that alcoholics can never control their drinking and, therefore, must never take another drop if they are to recover.

Complete abstinence is the goal of all members of AA, which is the most successful world-wide alcoholic treatment programme available. The number of the nearest branch can be found in the telephone directory and, if you consider you have a problem with alcohol, you can be sure to find a sympathetic audience.

Everybody there will understand your problem – they have all been there themselves. Basically, AA groups offer an alternative mood-altering process for those suffering from addictive diseases.

Q What are these Twelve Steps?

The Twelve Steps are a related number of vows and counsels of perfection that members make both to themselves and publicly in the group. The idea is that members work through the steps methodically at every meeting, discussing and interpreting them. Also, everybody encourages everybody else, and there are often celebrations to celebrate periods of sobriety. Sometimes there may be a birthday cake to celebrate a year's sobriety – something very much worth celebrating, as all alcoholics will agree.

The following are the Twelve Steps, along with a brief explanation.

Step One We admitted we were powerless over alcohol, that our lives had become unmanageable.

Explanation Most alcoholics are under the illusion that they are in control and can stop drinking at any time they like. This step asks people to admit the opposite, that the addiction is actually controlling them. This step allows them to face up to and admit the addiction.

Step Two We came to believe that a power greater than ourselves could restore us to sanity.

Explanation Many people find this step difficult, as it seems to require, in this secular age, a belief in a supernatural power. But all it need mean is that, at AA, people hand over to the power of the group, which is always greater than the individual. This step is also an acknowledgement that it is impossible to recover completely by ourselves and that we need help.

Step Three We made a decision to turn our will and

our lives over to the care of God *as we understood God*.

Explanation This can be interpreted as meaning that, at last we are willing to listen to the authentic voice within.

Step Four We made a searching and fearless moral inventory of ourselves.

Explanation This means that we do not have to blame ourselves, but only to come to terms with ourselves and understand our actions. We learn to stop blaming others and take responsibility at last.

Step Five We admitted to God, to ourselves, and to another human being the exact nature of our wrongs.

Explanation This step basically means that we replace dishonesty with honesty.

Step Six We were entirely ready to have God remove all these defects of character.

Explanation We do not have to believe in God to accept this step but we should be ready to let go of all the dysfunctional habits that have prolonged our alcoholism.

Step Seven We humbly asked Him to remove our shortcomings.

Explanation We now ask that all the defects of character should fall away, so that the genuine, pleasant person underneath can re-emerge.

Step Eight We made a list of all persons we had harmed, and became willing to make amends to them all.

Explanation All alcoholics, without execption, harm the lives of other people. The idea of this step is to put paid to all the shame and guilt we feel in connection with these people, and acknowledge that we have harmed others.

Step Nine We made direct amends to such people wherever possible, except when to do so would injure them or others.

Explanation We actually tell the people we have harmed that we realize what we have done and that we are sorry.

Step Ten We continued to take personal inventory, and when we were wrong promptly admitted it.

Explanation We acknowledge that we have to continue to be watchful and honest. AA realizes that habits cannot be broken in an instant and may take time.

Step Eleven We sought through prayer and meditation to improve our conscious contact with God *as we understood God*, praying only for knowledge of His will for us and the power to carry that out.

Explanation We have to remember to allow ourselves periods of quiet in order to continue in our sobriety.

Step Twelve Having had a spiritual awakening as a result of these steps, we tried to carry this message to others and to practise these principles in all our affairs.

Explanation We should not keep the message of hope, love and positivity to ourselves but, by our own example, let other people see that it is possible to become sober, to take responsibility, to make valid choices and free themselves from the stranglehold of alcoholic behaviour.

A more detailed explanation of these steps is available in the AA 'Big Book' (AA, 1993), which can be consulted at all branches. As you will see, only the first step mentions the word alcohol; the others are a guide for life to help people awaken the spiritual side of themselves.

Although AA is a successful means of recovering from alcoholism, many people object to the spiritual and religious aspect of these steps, and the rather evangelical nature of AA meetings.

Others use this as an excuse to continue their addictive behaviour. It takes a lot of courage to go to an initial AA meeting, and actually admit that you have a problem with drinking.

Q What types of treatment other than AA are available?

AA remains the most popular form of alcoholism therapy in the world, but there are other models of understanding, other approaches if you do not like the intensely spiritual leanings of AA. They operate on a different basis from AA, which basically believes that drinking for alcoholics is not a choice, that it is a progressive disease, and one which develops when there is profound alienation from the spirit, from the essence of the individual.

The *moral-volitional model* assumes that drinking is a mater of choice and that 'loss of control' arises from weakness or depravity. It must be said that very few psychologists now take this view, but it is the oldest model still alive and is the one adopted by the US Supreme Court. The assumption here is that you could stop drinking if you really wanted to.

The *personality model* emerged at the beginning of the twentieth century with the rise of psycho-analysis. It views alcoholism as an underlying personality problem arising from a disturbance of normal development during childhood and assumes that alcoholics share certain traits which are undesirable in adults.

In other words, alcoholics are stuck permanently at an adolescent or childish stage of development, a kind of grandiose or egotistical state where they have to take centre stage and be the most important person in any gathering. At the very least, by being alcoholics, they can draw attention to themselves.

In the *family system model*, an approach adopted by many psychiatrists working in NHS hospitals in the UK, alcoholism is seem as a family disorder, liable to develop when there is severe dysfunction within the family unit.

The play *Long Day's Journey into Night*, by Eugene O'Neill, powerfully evokes how drugs, alcohol and dysfunction all combine to produce a destructive and unhealthy family unit in which members cannot live together but, equally, cannot live apart, and all are deeply affected by the mind-altering substance which they use.

This play was very closely based on O'Neill's own early life. His father was an alcoholic, his mother was a drug-addict, he himself was also an alcoholic and his brother committed suicide during a severe drinking bout. O'Neill was the father of Oona

O'Neill, who married the 54-year-old Charlie Chaplin when only 18-years-old. She hardly knew her father, who played little part in her upbringing, but her brother also became alcoholic.

The *disposition disease model* developed in the USA with the repeal of Prohibition in 1933. (It is interesting to note that most of the principal models for alcohol attitudes and treatment began in the USA, which itself has been called the alcoholic republic of the world). This view is of alcoholism as a particular kind of disease with a biological, hereditary cause. It is considered to be a physical abnormality, causing inability to control consumption of alcohol after the first drink, and is a disease for which there is no cure. Therapy here is by detoxification followed by education about the disease process.

As with AA, the emphasis is on complete abstinence, in much the same way as diabetics must avoid certain foods because of the risk of going into a diabetic coma. This disease model of alcoholism is becoming increasingly popular as the idea of the condition being the result of moral weakness, which can be overcome by the addict 'pulling himself together', becomes less accepted.

Also popular, and successful for some, is the *cognitive-behavioural theory*, which takes the view that, as the alcoholic thought himself into drinking, so he can think himself out if it by changing his thinking patterns.

Person-centred counselling, developed by Carl Rogers in the USA, takes the view that everyone is an 'expert' in their own lives, and the therapist acts as a facilitator, rather than an expert, gradually and non-judgementally drawing the subjects out so that they can describe and admit the problem, come to terms with it, and then take personal responsibility for their future actions.

The *social-learning theory* is based on the idea that problem drinking is a cultural, learned behaviour, rather than an innate one.

All these models and approaches have some validity, and there is no overwhelmingly successful model or treatment approach which leads to sobriety in all cases.

Q Isn't there a drug you can take to stop drinking?

No, but there is a drug called Antabuse which works by producing an unpleasant effect if alcohol is taken. This helps people who are determined not to drink to stay away from alcohol. Within 15 minutes of taking alcohol, the active ingredient in the drug produces red eyes, a flushed face, throbbing headache, fast-beating heart, dizziness, nausea, sweating and vomiting. Convulsions and a drop in blood pressure may also occur. These effects last from 1 to several hours and, because of this, Antabuse should be started only under hospital supervision.

It should never be used by pregnant women and people with heart disease. There is a great deal of controversy surrounding Antabuse. Some addiction specialists swear by it as a simple and short-lasting treatment, while others believe that, at best, it creates a condition known as 'dry-drunk' – a state in which the former alcoholic no longer drinks, but continues to display all the personality disorders which were present when he was drinking. In other words, as with all drugs, this one treats the symptoms and not the underlying disorder.

The most successful use of Antabuse seems to be by ex-alcoholics who have achieved abstinence but want the 'insurance' of the drug in case they come up against a risky situation. Its successful use as part of a closely supervised in-patient or out-patient treatment régime has been reported.

Q Is it ever possible for an alcoholic to drink in moderation after recovery?

Members of AA groups say quite definitely: 'No. Those who become alcoholics are, actually, no good at drinking and can never learn to do it sensibly'. Beauchamp Colcough, a psychologist specializing in the treatment of compulsive disorders and a recovering alcoholic himself, believes that asking an alcoholic to drink in moderation is like asking a compulsive wife-beater to beat his wife in moderation.

For alcoholics, drinking will always be wrong, because they cannot do it sensibly.

Recently, though, newer treatment models have questioned this complete insistence on abstinence. Alcohol Concern has details of programmes which teach moderate drinking. At the moment, this remains highly controversial and a majority of recovering alcoholics would maintain that controlled drinking after detoxification is actually impossible, as alcoholism is an incurable disease treatable only by avoiding the substance which caused the problem in the first place.

The proponents of controlled drinking agree that most chronic drinkers will only succeed if they abstain, but many serious drinkers, especially younger people, actually do better if they do not aim for long-term abstinence.

Q I have heard the term 'enabler' connected with alcoholism. What does this mean?

Very often, those who live with and work around alcoholics try to cover up the addict's drinking by pretending that it is not happening, e.g.by hiding bottles and giving them money, so that the alcoholic is prevented from facing the consequences of his or her actions. It is extremely common for alcoholics to marry other alcoholics, so that the two collude in the bad behaviour.

In some treatment centres, the partner or other enabler is treated along with the active alcoholic in order to break the destructive habits which have built up over many years. It also has to be understood that alcoholics often come from addictive family backgrounds, so that alcoholism will seem normal to them, even though life with a compulsive drinker is always uncomfortable.

Robin Norwood's book, *Women Who Love Too Much*, consists mainly of case histories of women who had married alcoholics or other abusive men, and not only continually covered up for them but actually sought them out, believing them to be more 'exciting' or 'glamorous' than sober or non-addicted males.

Other terms used for enabler are 'co-alcoholic' and 'co-dependent'.

Q What is the Minnesota Model, and how does it work?

This treatment is based on the AA Twelve Step programme, but takes the whole idea much further.
Again, the goal is total and permanent abstinence
from mood-altering and addictive substances.

Minnesota Model treatment centres, e.g. the Betty
Ford Clinic in the USA, are almost always
residential and introduce patients to the Twelve
Steps at the same time as offering detoxification.

This model differs from other detoxification
centres in trying to involve the family in the
recovery process by helping them to understand
what addiction is all about, and why all family
members are affected by it.

During treatment and therapy, family members learn
not to 'enable' by hiding bottles of drink, paying
for drinks, covering up or concealing the truth. The
parents, children, and partners of active alcoholics
are helped to see the part they have played in the
process, and that it is not a matter of a saint and a
sinner – all have colluded and covered up.

As the problem has usually been denied for many
years, therapy may be difficult and prolonged. The
spouse or other family member must want the

alcoholic to recover, and be committed to turning dysfunctional relationships into healthy and functional ones.

Minnesota Model centres differ from AA meetings in that they are staffed by qualified counsellors, therapists and doctors. They are not self-help organizations, but places where alcoholics and their families can learn all about the dynamics of the disease, ask questions and increase their understanding of the disease process.

Q **But don't family members always want the alcoholic to recover?**

Surprising as this may seem, the answer is no, not always. In many cases, a highly complicated lifestyle has been built around the alcoholic, and family members have not only learned to cope, they actually like it, in spite of their protestations to the contrary.

As the Minnesota Model treatment centres progressed, it was learned that partners of alcoholics were by no means always grateful when the drink problem appeared to be resolved. Originally, it was expected that partners would be overwhelmed with delight, but not a bit of it! It appeared that some families coped far better with an alcoholic in their midst.

In recovery, the formerly using member often seemed to have become dull and characterless, even boring. Relationships are not always strengthened with sobriety — sometimes they break up.

One of the toughest aspects of family therapy is that all members have to take responsibility for the part they may have played in the alcoholic's behaviour — and be prepared to change. During therapy, it often emerges that the only attractive or engaging aspect of the alcoholic was that he drank. In recovery, he becomes a different person.

Also, when there is an alcoholic in the family, it is easy for the others to feel superior and saintly. It is uncomfortable for members to recognize that they may have been less than saintly themselves and, although not to blame for the drinking problem, have not helped matters.

Minnesota Model treatment centres ask everybody dealing with the alcoholic to examine their own behaviour carefully as well. In many cases, multi-generational dysfunction will be uncovered and, for all, recovery constitutes a steep and sometimes uncomfortable learning curve.

It would be wonderful if alcoholics could just take a pill and stop drinking so that there would be no need for all this fuss. Unfortunately, alcoholism is such a very complicated disease that there are no simple roads to recovery. If there were, they would probably have been discovered by now, as the problem is as old as time.

The point about the kind of treatment offered at Minnesota centres is that, through the talking cure, through therapy and counselling, the rot can stop, and unhealthy relationships be replaced by healthy ones. In the end, alcoholism does no one any favours – and there are no simple answers to effective recovery.

Q I have heard of 'tough love', but what does it mean?

This is part of the Minnesota Model of recovery, whereby alcoholics or other addicts have to face the consequences of their own actions. This means that alcoholics who drink while in treatment are turned out. If they have no money to get home, that's their fault – they have broken the agreed rules and must abide by the consequences. It is often difficult, if not impossible, for families to see alcoholics suffer and not give them a drink when they cry out and plead for one, and this is one reason why going to a treatment centre can be the only way to recovery.

Q Does treatment work?

The treatment works if the patients abide by the rules but, unfortunately, backsliding from any addiction is extremely common. A success rate of 60 per cent for residential treatment is usually considered excellent and there is no treatment which can be absolutely guaranteed. If people really want to change, then most can, but if they don't there is nothing anybody can do to make them.

Q Are private treatment centres very expensive?

Yes, about twice as much as going to a major private school. But most have bursary funds and sliding scales for those in difficulties. Also, many schemes are available on private health insurance, as alcoholism has at last come to be recognized as a serious and treatable disease rather than something to be hidden away and denied.

Q What are halfway houses?

These are places, usually residential, where alcoholics and other addicts can go after detoxification and a certain amount of therapy. Halfway houses have a more relaxed régime than treatment centres, which offer full-time therapy and treatment and, in some cases, residents can go to work or carry on a reasonably normal life while still attending therapy and counselling sessions.

Halfway houses are designed for people for whom recovery is difficult, and who need a little more time in a somewhat sheltered environment before venturing fully into the outside world./They are for the people who do not feel sufficiently confident of their ability to cope on their own, but who have detoxified and withdrawn, and for whom full-time treatment is no longer appropriate.

Length of stay at halfway houses is determined by levels of confidence, self-esteem and recovery, and may be several weeks or even months. Again, clients are usually turned out if they are caught drinking – and if they have nowhere to go, that is their fault. It is 'tough love' in action, designed to stop the process whereby others collude in the drinking behaviour and forgive and forget time and again.

Q What other help is available for family members?

An increasing number of facilities are becoming available. For many years, A1-Anon and A1-Ateen have provided meeting places for partners and family members of active alcoholics. They run parallel with AA meetings and are available world-wide.

Newer organizations, run on similar lines, exist for the Adult Children of Alcoholics, who may or may not themselves be using alcohol. Whether they are or not, it is now recognized that children growing up in the homes of alcoholics exhibit many personality problems which they carry into adult life, without realizing the part alcohol has played. The most overwhelming characteristic of the children of alcoholics is that they have never been allowed to be themselves. Instead of the parents being there for the children, it has been the other way round, with the children often having to take responsibility for the alcoholic's behaviour.

Instead of interest being centred round them, as should happen, all the interest and attention has gone to alcohol. This leads such children to grow up in a variety of ways in which they are all paying roles rather than being themselves.

Some children will be cast into the role of hero or heroine – the one whose job it is to save the family and thus prove that they were not so bad after all. Other roles are the scapegoat, the naughty child who is always blamed when things go wrong, and the aloof one, the child who separates himself or herself from the family and has as little to do with them as possible.

People who feel their lives have been affected by

having an alcoholic in the family – which most often shows itself in an inability to form proper relationships in adult life – can go along to meetings, where they will meet others like themselves and, through the talking cure, come to an understanding of the patterns of behaviour and how these can be changed.

There are also growing networks of meetings for co-dependents, or co-alcoholics, as they used to be called. Accept, an American-based alcoholism recovery centre in London, UK, offers all kinds of therapy and approaches for family members, as well as active alcohol users, and there is no fee of any kind charged.

There may be some modest fees at the various 'Anonymous' organizations, but they are very small and usually intended just to cover the cost of hiring a hall, tea and coffee, etc.

In addition to this, a growing number of private therapists offer treatment and advice for those who feel their lives have been ruined by having an alcoholic in the family.

It should be said that, initially, therapy and treatment may be painful, but those who have had the courage to face their problems agree that it has been worthwhile; the resulting feeling is like a big dark cloud rolling away and being replaced by sunlight and sunny uplands.

Generally speaking, it is difficult for those affected by another's alcoholism to recover by themselves without group therapy or professional help. This is because alcoholism isolates everybody who comes into contact with it and, before treatment, family members may well have been unable to talk about the problem with anybody else.

The relief that comes from being able to bring the subject out into the open, to discuss and face the problem, is tremendous.

Q Is there any way of preventing alcoholism?

Yes. Don't drink every day, don't drink too much and don't use alcohol to hide from feelings.

Q Can a person ever be said to have recovered from alcoholism?

According to AA and its various offshoots, the answer to this is no. For this reason, some people continue going to AA meetings for years, several times a week. Eternal vigilance is necessary, if only because of the many lifestyle, personality and behavioural problems that alcohol abuse causes. For some people, recovery is a lifelong process. Of course, not everybody who recovers from alcoholism will want to examine deeply all the personal issues involved. Some just want to stop drinking, not to spend years in analysis or self-searching. For others, though, stopping drinking becomes the start of an interesting inner journey which becomes ever more fascinating as time goes on.

You might imagine that, if you go to AA meetings several times a week, you will become intensely selfish and pre-occupied. In fact, the opposite happens. Nobody is more selfish than an alcoholic, who systematically destroys not only his own life and well-being but that of everybody close to him. Through going to AA, or other self-help groups, the alcoholic, who formerly only lived for himself and his drinking, will come to have a proper regard for other people.

Some people do recover from alcoholism and discontinue going to AA meetings. Not everybody has to go to AA in order to separate alcohol permanently from their lives.

Q What happens if I find myself in a situation where drink is being pressed on me?

This happens to all recovering alcoholics, who may be seen as less fun, less jolly, once they have given up drinking. Erstwhile drinking companions cannot be expected to encourage a former alcoholic not to drink when they are drinking themselves, so they will do all they can to persuade him to be in the same boat as themselves.

In extreme cases, recovering alcoholics may have to change their social companions. This is often an additional problem: their social lives, which revolved around drink, have disappeared and they may have to change the venues which they frequent. Most counsellors for alcohol problems advise former alcohol-abusers to avoid places which sell alcoholic beverages as much as possible, so as to make permanent the break between being a drinker and a non-drinker.

5 Life After Alcoholism

Q **How will life be better without drink?**

When you are a confirmed drinker, you may imagine that life will be impossible without drink. How will you enjoy a party? How will you talk to people? How will you get through a dinner party? Here, the philosophy of AA can come in handy: take it one day at a time. Of course there will be times when you miss drink – after all, it has become your best friend, and losing it will initially be like a bereavement, as is releasing yourself from any addiction.

But gradually, you will find that you regain yourself, your family and most of all, your self-respect. You will be able to make better relationships, ones which are not clouded by alcohol, and you will be able to face the future with less fear and terror than before.

Remember, an alcoholic is basically a person who is frightened of life, frightened of himself and frightened of the future. That is one reason for the chaotic drinking – to blot out clear perception, anxiety and worry.

You will probably also find that your financial situation improves because alcoholism is an expensive habit, however rich you may be.

Q Which is the 'real' me – the alcoholic one or the sober one?

There is no doubt about his – the sober one. Although there is an old proverb, in *vino veritas*, all this really means is that sometimes what appears to be the truth can come out when inhibitions are shed. But the 'real' person is always the non-addicted one. It is impossible to be real when you are addicted to a mind-altering chemical.

A certain very talented journalist had two distinct personalities: a sober one and an alcoholic one. When sober, he was rather shy, diffident and brusque but, when drunk, he became expansive, extrovert, witty and warm. Most people preferred the drunken version and, indeed, he had turned to alcohol in the first place because he did not like himself sober.

As the years went by, however, his drinking became so out of control that he had no idea what effect it would have. Sometimes he could drink a lot and apparently be able to conduct his day-to-day life quite normally, while at other times he would become completely drunk with a tot or two of whisky.

Eventually, his life became unbearable and he decided to go to a treatment centre. He learned that his treatment would cost £7,000 (about $11,000) but considered that it was worth it. He went up to the door – then decided he would try and live without alcohol in future.

He hasn't touched a drop since and his 'real' personality has settled down somewhere between his former sober gruffness and alcoholic expansiveness. He started drinking in the first place to give himself confidence, but then realized that alcohol actually took away his confidence because, in the end, he became so addicted he could not pick up the phone, talk to anybody or go home from work before having a drink.

He still smokes heavily and gives as his justification that he must have some addiction in his life. Many alcoholics at treatment centres continue to smoke. Although this is not encouraged, it is seen as the least mind-altering of addictive substances.

Q How will my health improve?

The first thing that you will notice is that you start to sleep better. Alcoholics are very bad sleepers, and become accustomed to not having a good night's sleep. We need sleep in order to regenerate body systems, to dream and to rest the brain, mind and emotions, and anybody who is chronically short of sleep will find that this leads to other diseases.

Your skin tone will improve very quickly and you may find that your digestion improves markedly as well. But there may well be a 'healing crisis' where things get worse before they get better. There may be days when you feel desperate for a drink, especially at low points.

But this longing will pass and, as your general health and energy levels pick up, you will not want to ruin them again by going back to drinking.

Q If I have been sober for a very long time, can't I just have a couple of drinks?

This does seem very tempting, especially on occasions such as Christmas or a wedding, when everybody else is drinking. Also, whatever people may say about non-alcoholic beverages, they are not the ideal accompaniment to food and they don't really make you want to continue drinking, as alcohol does.

But most recovering alcoholics maintain that, for somebody who is addicted to alcohol, there is no such thing as a couple of drinks. This may seem very harsh advice, but it comes from those who have tried it and know it doesn't work.

Beauchamp Colclough, author of The Effective Way to Stop Drinking, says: 'For someone who is addicted to alcohol, there is no such thing as a couple of drinks. There never was a couple of drinks, so why should there be now? If you pick up a drink again, you're picking up the nightmare – only there's a twist in it. You don't pick up where you left off. You'll be plunged very quickly into a dark hole, because that's the only direction in which your addiction will lead you.'

For alcoholics, will-power is not the issue – they simply cannot control their drinking any more than, by thinking, a short-sighted person can re-gain normal sight. Somebody with short sight will always have to wear glasses to normalize their vision, and most addicted drinkers will always have to abstain to remain in control.

It seems that the only people who can learn to drink sensibly are those who, while they may have drunk heavily at times in the past, are not actually alcoholics by nature.

Q Will I be able to form proper relationships after recovery?

There is far more chance of this. During active alcoholism it is impossible to form good relation-ships, intimate, familial or professional, because so much of the personality is shut down or un-available. In some cases, original relationships can improve, but it is far more likely that the recovering alcoholic will form a new set of relationships with entirely new people.

At the same time, your existing family relationships may improve dramatically, even if, perhaps, a marriage ends, because you will take responsibility and not automatically blame other people for what happens to you.

Most recovering alcoholics have no doubt in their minds that life is far better when they are not chemically addicted, and that it is only once they become free from the effects of the substance that they are able to form proper relationships.

As alcohol has such a devastating effect on the brain and personality, there is every chance that all aspects of a good relationship will become possible after sobriety is achieved. It may take some time, as alcoholics will have become used to dysfunction, deviousness and deceit in their relationships.

But it does seem that, on the whole, alcoholics are often very sensitive and perceptive and, frequently, people are surprised at what a very pleasant person emerges when the dependency on drink can be overcome. In so many cases, it is the drink rather than the underlying personality which has turned a basically decent person into somebody to avoid.

Useful Addresses

Self-help Groups

Australia

Marketing Division
Alcohol and Drug Foundation
Australia
P O Box 269
Woden
ACT 2606

Provides a Directory of Services
for Alcoholism.

New Zealand

The Alcoholic Liquor Advisory
Council
P O Box 5023
Wellington

Publishes the Directory of
Addiction Services in New
Zealand.

South Africa

South African National Council
on Alcoholism and Drug
Dependence
P O Box 10134
Braamfontein 2001

Gives information on services
available

United Kingdom

Al-Anon Family Groups
61 Great Dover Street
London SE1 4YF
Tel. 0171 403 0888

Alcoholics Anonymous
P O Box 1
Stonebow House
Stonebow
York YO1 2NJ
Tel. 01604 644 026
London office
Tel. 0171 352 3001

Useful Addresses

The National Association for Children of Alcoholics
P O Box 64
Fishponds
Bristol BS16 2UE
Tel. 0800 289 0611

All these groups have 12-step programmes and branches all over the United Kingdom.

United States of America

Adult Children of Alcoholics
P O Box 3216
2522 W. Sepulveda Boulevard
Suite 200
Torrance
California 90505
Tel. 213 534 1815

Professional Services

United Kingdom

ACCEPT
724 Fulham Road
London SW6 5SE
Tel. 0171 371 7477

Provides a range of services for alcoholics.

Alcohol Concern
Waterbridge House
32–36 Loman Street
London SE1 0EE
Tel. 0171 928 7377

Offers a comprehensive list of alcohol agencies. Also publishes a quarterly magazine, and details, prices and treatment methods of most alcohol treatment centres.

Alcohol Services Directory
Dolomite Publishing
Freepost G1/2775
107 Kings Road
Godalming
Surrey GU7 3BR
Tel. 01483 421 027

Publishes the most
comprehensive directory of
alcohol services in the UK.

Drinkline
(National Alcohol Helpline)
Tel. (London)   0171 332 0202
    (All UK)   01345 320 202
operates
Monday–Friday 9.30am–11pm,
Saturday and Sunday 6pm–11pm

The Drug and Alcohol
Foundation
15 Allington Street
London SW1E 5EB
Tel. 0171 828 2675

Greater London Association of
Alcohol Services
330-331 Great Sutton Street
London EC1V 0DX
Tel. 0171 253 6221

St Joseph's Centre for Addiction
Holy Cross Hospital
Hindhead Road
Haslemere
Surrey GU27 1NQ
Tel. 01428 656 517

A wide range of services is
available, including in-patient
detoxification and rehabilitation.

Turning Point
New Loom House
101 Back Church Lane
London E1 1LU
Tel. 0171 022 300

Treats around 12,000 people a
year in a range of day-care and
residential projects.

Women's Alcohol Centre
66a Drayton Park
London N5 1ND
Tel. 0171 226 4581

Free counselling, day- and
residential care.

References

Alcoholics Anonymous (1993) *Alcoholics Anonymous* 3rd
  edition. Alcoholics Anonymous

Beauchamp, C (1993) *The Effective Way to Stop Drinking.*
  Penguin

Buess, L (1989) *Children of Light, Children of Denial.* Light
  Technology

Cruse, J (1989) *Painful Affairs.* Health Communications

Kent, R (1989) *Drinking Problems.* Sheldon Press

McGonville, B (1985) *Women under the Influence: Alcohol and its
  Impact.* Virago

Norwood, R (1989) *Women Who Love Too Much.* Century

Royal College of Psychiatrists (1986) *Alcohol: Our Favourite
  Drug.* Tavistock

Sweet, C (1994) *Off the Hook: How to Break Free from Addiction and
  Enjoy a New Life.* Piatkus

Stafford, D (1992) *Children of Alcoholics: How a Parent's Drinking
  can Affect your Life.* Piatkus

Index

Index